Weightlifting & Strength Building

An Integrated Life of Fitness

Core Workouts

Cross-Training

Eating Right & Additional Supplements for Fitness

Endurance & Cardio Training

Exercise for Physical & Mental Health

Flexibility & Agility

Sports & Fitness

Step Aerobics & Aerobic Dance

Weightlifting & Strength Building

Yoga & Pilates

An Integrated Life of Fitness

Weightlifting & Strength Building

CELICIA SCOTT

Mason Crest

Mason Crest
450 Parkway Drive, Suite D
Broomall, PA 19008
www.masoncrest.com

Printed and bound in the United States of America.

First printing
9 8 7 6 5 4 3 2 1

Series ISBN: 978-1-4222-3156-2
Hardcover ISBN: 978-1-4222-3165-4
Paperback ISBN: 978-1-4222-3203-3
ebook ISBN: 978-1-4222-8703-3

Cataloging-in-Publication Data on file with the Library of Congress.

CONTENTS

Introduction   6

1. Lifting Weights, Building Strength   9

2. Weight-Training Equipment   23

3. Nutrition for Strength   33

4. Making a Plan to
   Build Strength with Weightlifting   43

Find Out More   58

Series Glossary of Key Terms   60

Index   62

About the Author and the Consultant
   & Picture Credits   64

KEY ICONS TO LOOK FOR:

Text-Dependent Questions: These questions send the reader back to the text for more careful attention to the evidence presented there.

Words to Understand: These words with their easy-to-understand definitions will increase the reader's understanding of the text, while building vocabulary skills.

Series Glossary of Key Terms: This back-of-the book glossary contains terminology used throughout this series. Words found here increase the reader's ability to read and comprehend higher-level books and articles in this field.

Research Projects: Readers are pointed toward areas of further inquiry connected to each chapter. Suggestions are provided for projects that encourage deeper research and analysis.

Sidebars: This boxed material within the main text allows readers to build knowledge, gain insights, explore possibilities, and broaden their perspectives by weaving together additional information to provide realistic and holistic perspectives.

INTRODUCTION

Choosing fitness as a priority in your life is one of the smartest decisions you can make! This series of books will give you the tools you need to understand how your decisions about eating, sleeping, and physical activity can affect your health now and in the future.

And speaking of the future: YOU are the future of our world. We who are older are depending on you to build something wonderful—and we, as lifelong advocates of good nutrition and physical activity, want the best for you throughout your whole life.

Our hope in these books is to support and guide you to instill healthy behaviors beginning today. You are in a unique position to adopt healthy habits that will guide you toward better health right now and avoid health-related problems as an adult.

You have the power of choice today. We recognize that it's a very busy world filled with overwhelming choices that sometimes get in the way of you making wise decisions when choosing food or in being active. But no previous training or skills are needed to put this material into practice right away.

We want you to have fun and build your confidence as you read these books. Your self-esteem will increase. LEARN, EXPLORE, and DIS-COVER, using the books as your very own personal guide. A tremendous amount of research over the past thirty years has proven that the quality of your health and life will depend on the decisions you make today that affect your body, mind, and inner self.

You are an individual, liking different foods, doing different things, having different interests, and growing up in different families. But you are not alone as you face these vital decisions in your life. Those of us in the fitness professions are working hard to get healthier foods into your schools; to make sure you have an opportunity to be physically active on a regular basis; to ensure that walking and biking are encouraged in your communities; and to build communities where healthy, affordable foods can be purchased close to home. We're doing all we can to support you. We've got your back!

Moving step by step to healthier eating habits and increasing physical activity requires change. Change happens in small steps, so be patient with yourself. Change takes time. But get started *now*.

Lead an "action-packed" life! Your whole body will thank you by becoming stronger and healthier. You can look and do your best. You'll feel good. You'll have more energy. You'll reap the benefits of smart lifestyle choices for a healthier future so you can achieve what's important to you.

Choose to become the best you can be!

—Diana H. Hart, President
National Association for Health and Fitness

Words to Understand

prestigious: Widely recognized and admired.

Chapter One

LIFTING WEIGHTS, BUILDING STRENGTH

If you've never thought about weight training, it may seem a little scary. But you don't have to be an Olympic weight lifter rippling with enormous muscles to benefit from this form of fitness.

Not only does weightlifting make you feel strong and improve your health, but it also makes you look slimmer and more toned and athletic. Here are some of its benefits:

- It builds up muscle strength, making muscles and joints less likely to be injured or diseased.

Lifting weights is one of the best ways to build strength and muscle, but it has many other health benefits as well.

Weightlifting & Strength Building

Make Connections

 Aerobic exercise gives our hearts and lungs a workout. The term aerobic actually means "with oxygen," indicating that this kind of exercise depends on getting extra oxygen to the muscles to help them move. Anaerobic exercise, on the other hand, depends more on burning glycogen, a form of sugar. The word anaerobic means "without oxygen," so this kind of exercise doesn't get you breathing as hard. Weightlifting is considered anaerobic exercise—but by making your muscles stronger, it can also help you do better at aerobic forms of exercise.

- When combined with a proper diet, it helps you to lose weight. Each pound of muscle in your body burns up thirty to forty calories a day. The more muscle you have, the more fat you lose.
- Weight training is a great way to control stress. It releases "feel-good" chemicals in your body called endorphins, which give you a sense of well-being.
- It can make you physically stronger and more capable of safely handling heavy loads.
- It will help you perform better in other sports, boosting aerobic fitness and muscular power.

MUSCLE DEVELOPMENT

Your body has more than six hundred muscles. Each muscle is built up of tiny fibers called myofibrils. When you need to perform a task requiring muscle power, your brain sends electrical orders to the muscle fibers through your nerve cells (also called neurons). The muscle fibers

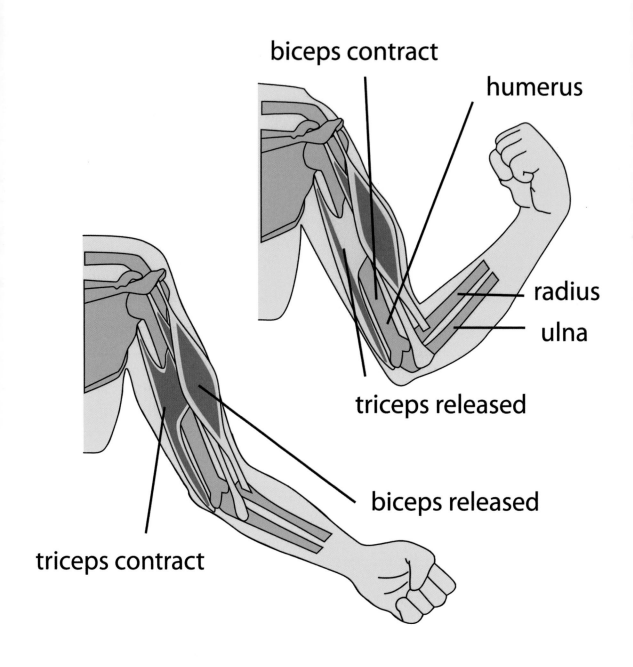

biceps contract

humerus

radius

ulna

triceps released

biceps released

triceps contract

With each movement you make, your muscles contract and expand. Each muscle has a specific function in the body.

Weight training pushes your muscles to grow bigger and stronger the more you work them out.

contract or relax according to the orders they receive from the brain. This contracting (getting shorter) and expanding (getting longer) is what makes your muscles pull your bones, making your body move.

Weight training results in improved strength and muscle bulk for several different reasons. First, the myofibrils respond to the weight training by growing thicker and stronger. Second, the actual number of myofibrils increases, expanding the size and power of the muscle. Finally, weight training improves the communication between the brain and the muscles.

Lifting Weights, Building Strength   13

Weightlifting has a long history as an Olympic sport. Here, French weightlifter Roger Francois competes in the 1928 Olympic Games in Amsterdam.

Weightlifting & Strength Building

We acquire any skill through practice, and doing weight training makes us more familiar with our bodies, giving us the balance, strength, and focus needed to lift heavy objects. For this reason alone, beginners at weight training develop additional strengths even before their muscles have started to grow.

WEIGHTLIFTING AS A SPORT

Weight training as a sport started back in the late nineteenth century. Gyms spread throughout Europe and the United States. The International Weightlifting Federation (IWF), based in Budapest, was founded in 1905. Today, the IWF controls the competitive sport of weightlifting.

Weightlifting became an Olympic sport in 1920. Women have also entered weightlifting. In 1987, the first all-female World Championship was held, and women's weightlifting became an Olympic sport in 2000.

In Olympic weightlifting, participants attempt a maximum weight single lift of a barbell loaded with weight plates. The two lifts competed are the "clean and jerk" and the "snatch."

- The snatch involves lifting a weight straight from the floor to above the head in one movement. As the bar is lifted, the weightlifter drops down into a squatting position under the bar, while locking his arms to support the weights above him. Finally, he pushes himself up from the squatting position to a final standing position and holds the weight for a required length of time before lowering it.
- The clean and jerk differs because the weightlifter must first transfer the bar to shoulder height as he moves to the squatting position. This is the "clean" part of the technique. The "jerk" comes when the weightlifter pushes up with his legs and thrusts the weight above his head.

In both cases, the judges are looking for good technique as well as the heaviest weight lifted. Any errors in technique will result in points being deducted.

Women from around the world have been competing in Olympic weightlifting since 2000.

Weightlifting & Strength Building

Competitors compete in one of eight (seven for women) divisions determined by their body mass. In each weight division, competitors compete in both the snatch and the clean and jerk. Prizes are usually given for the heaviest weights lifted in the snatch, clean and jerk, and the two combined.

The order of the competition is up to the lifters: the competitor who chooses to attempt the lowest weight goes first. If he is unsuccessful at that weight, he has the option of reattempting that lift or trying a heavier weight later (after any other competitors have made attempts at that weight or any intermediate weights). Weights are set in 1-kilogram increments, and each lifter can have a maximum of three lifts, regardless of whether lifts are successful or not.

The title "best lifter" is commonly awarded at local competitions. The award is based on the lifters' Sinclair Coefficients, which calculate strength-to-weight ratio of the lifters. Typically, the winner of the heaviest weight class will have lifted the most weight, but a winner in a lighter weight class will have lifted more in proportion to his body weight.

Weightlifting is not a sport recommended for young people under eighteen years old. The strain it places on the muscles and skeleton is huge. The world's greatest weightlifters can haul over 440 pounds above their heads, but even weights a quarter of that should not be attempted by the young or the untrained. Weightlifters must also be extremely fit, as well as very strong. During each lift, the heart rate is pushed as high as 200 beats per minute, a dangerous level for those without advanced aerobic fitness.

BODYBUILDING

Bodybuilding is another competitive sport that developed out of weight-lifting. In 1939, the first Mr. American competition was held under the auspices of the Amateur Athletic Union. Competitive bodybuilding went

Mr. Olympia 2007 Ronnie Coleman poses for judges during a 2010 bodybuilding competition.

Weightlifting & Strength Building

international in 1946 when Ben and Joe Weider—whose surname is often seen on weights and weight equipment—formed the International Federation of Body Building (IFBB). The IFBB promoted the art of body-building in world competitions, including the **prestigious** Mr. Olympia and Mrs. Olympia. Bodybuilding is not yet an Olympic event, although the international Olympic Committee is becoming more accepting of the sport.

Bodybuilding became popular as a sport in the United States in the 1930s, and has since grown into a massive international competitive activity, as well as a multimillion dollar industry. Both men and women practice the sport, many dreaming of becoming Mr. or Ms. Olympia, the supreme title in all bodybuilding.

A bodybuilding competition lets athletes demonstrate their muscle development in front of a panel of judges. In international competi-tions, under the IFBB, there are nine judges. Each competitor must perform "mandatory poses"—in other words, poses that they must dis-play. There are seven mandatory poses for men and five for women. The poses are designed to display the six main muscle groups of the human body: arms, chest, abdomen, shoulders, backs, and legs. The bodybuilding is judged and scored according to four qualities: muscle definition, muscle density, muscle mass, and balanced muscu-lar development.

Bodybuilding competitions are as much about art as strength. Men are obliged to shave their bodies of any hair concealing their muscles. Tanning products and oils are also used to highlight the contours of the body. Taking part in bodybuilding competitions requires a great deal of dedication. Several hours of training, for at least three days a week, are essential.

The opportunities to take part in bodybuilding competitions are huge. A large number of local, national, and international bodybuild-ing organizations exist and promote their own competitions. Your club, gym, or coach should be able to point you in the direction of beginners' competitions. If not, any good bodybuilding magazine provides a competition calendar.

POWERLIFTING

Bodybuilding is about the appearance of the athletes. Weightlifting is about sheer strength. And powerlifting is a fusion of bodybuilding and weightlifting. The sport originated in bodybuilding gyms in the 1960s, when body builders began to compete for who could lift the heaviest weight. Today, powerlifting is an international sport, overseen by the International Powerlifting Federation (IPF).

There are three lifts in powerlifting: the bench press, squat, and dead lift. Like weightlifting, powerlifting is suitable only for adult competitors whose bodies have stopped growing. However, if you are interested in either sport, visit powerlifting or weightlifting websites or read magazines for more information about upcoming competitions. Watching competitions can teach you a lot about technique and etiquette, even if you are not training in the sport.

If, when you reach the right age for training, you are still interested in weightlifting or powerlifting, find a good team affiliated with a proper professional body such as U.S.A. Wrestling and International Powerlifting Federation.

WEIGHTLIFTING FOR EXERCISE

You don't need to be training as a professional, however, to enjoy some of the benefits of weightlifting. Weightlifting helps boost your strength, muscle definition, and energy levels. It also helps improve the density of your bones, which will make them strong and healthy for a lifetime. It's one path to a lifetime of fitness!

Words to Understand

comprehensive: Complete; covering all aspects of something.

abdominals: The muscles covering your stomach and intestines.

lats: A pair of large muscles covering the lower back.

pectorals: The muscles in the upper chest.

hydraulic: Using fluid to exert force.

resistance: Pushing back against something.

reps: The number of times you do an exercise in a row, without resting.

motivation: Your reason for doing something.

Chapter Two

WEIGHT-TRAINING EQUIPMENT

Weight training does not necessarily require weights. Much good work can be done through age-old techniques such as push-ups, crunches, and triceps dips. These have the big advantage that you can do them anywhere: in your living room, bedroom, or yard. Repeated every day in increasing numbers, such exercises will result in a strong body. The muscle development using weightless exercises, however, is generally neither as fast nor as **comprehensive** as training using weights. There are two systems of weights in strength training—free weights or weight machines.

Free weights can be small dumbbells like this or barbells lifted while standing or lying on an exercise bench.

FREE WEIGHTS

Free weights are simply heavy disks of metal (or, sometimes, weighted plastic), attached to a bar for lifting. There are generally two types of

Weightlifting & Strength Building

free weights: a dumbbell, which is designed to be held in one hand, and a long barbell, which is held in both hands. Combined with an exercise bench—a long, narrow bench, where you can lie or sit while lifting—free weights offer an option for successful weight training.

Free weights have their pros and cons. The pros are:

- A huge number of different exercises can be performed with the most basic set of free weights.
- Free weights are excellent for working individual muscles.
- Free weights are far less expensive to buy than weight machines.

Free weights also have some disadvantages, however:

- They are more difficult to use properly than weight machines because they require good balance. This means you are more likely to injure yourself using free weights if you have not been trained in the correct technique.
- Doing free weights on your own can be dangerous: you run the risk of dropping them on yourself.

WEIGHT MACHINES

The alternative to free weights is weight machines. Weight machines are pieces of equipment scientifically designed to work specific groups

Weight machines can be a great change from lifting free weights.

Weightlifting & Strength Building

of muscles. Therefore, there are weight machines for **abdominals**, **lats**, **pectorals**, and thigh muscles, along with others. A weight machine usually features a stack of weights, though some use systems of **hydraulic resistance** instead. For weight-stack machines, you select the weight you want to lift, pull, or push by putting a pin into a notch on the side of the stack.

Weight machines can be simple or extremely sophisticated. Some even alter the resistance according to how tired your muscles become as you go through a set of **reps**. Other advantages include:

- They usually feature more weight options than free weights, so you can pick the level at which you want to train.
- They are safer to use because they are designed to hold you securely while training. You can usually lift more because you do not have to worry about balance.
- You do not need a spotter; if you are having problems lifting a weight, the machine will let you lower it safely to rest.

If you are trying to decide between weight machines and free weights, then don't—use both. Combining the two ensures a well-rounded physique and an endless variety of exercises.

HOME OR GYM?

Weight training can be done at home or in a local gym. Home training is very convenient; you can train whenever you want to, without having to travel. However, for someone new to weight training, the disadvantages of training at home outweigh the advantages.

Home training is often done unsupervised, so there is a greater danger of injuring yourself by using poor technique or the wrong type of equipment, or by lifting weights that are too heavy for you. Also, you have the expense of setting up a home gym. Simple free weights can be bought relatively inexpensively, but add on the weight bench and

At a gym you can get help from trainers who know the proper way to lift and can keep you motivated to push yourself.

Weightlifting & Strength Building

Make Connections

Look inside a gym before you join. The quality of its staff, equipment, and surroundings has an impact on your safety when you are training, so check the following points:

- Is the gym clean and well kept? Remember to also look in the showers and changing areas.
- Are all the pieces of gym equipment in good condition? Are free weights stacked in order of weight? Look out for things such as torn seating or frayed cables on the weight machines.
- Is the gym using weight machines made by reputable brands, such as Bodymaster or Nautilus? If you are not familiar with the names, ask a sports professional (such as an assistant in a professional sports shop) about them.
- Are the free weights free of rust?
- Is the atmosphere inside the gym friendly but disciplined?

you might spend several hundred dollars. A complete weight machine center will easily cost you $800 to $1,000.

Another disadvantage is that people who train at home are more likely to give up. Exercising at home can be lonely and does not provide the *motivation* that comes from training around large groups of people.

Using a school or private gym solves these problems. A modern, well-equipped gym will contain a mix of both free weights and weight machines. There will also be experts within the gym to advise on safe and effective technique. Most gyms will make you go through a short introductory course to teach you the basics of how to use the equipment.

No matter where you choose to work out, lifting weights is a great way to get in shape and build strength.

Weightlifting & Strength Building

Some schools and colleges have gyms that are free of charge to the students.

Whether you choose to exercise at home or in a local gym, weight training is an excellent discipline to get you fit and in shape. "Discipline," however, is an important word. Your mind must be as fit and controlled as your body in order to get the most out of weight training.

Words to Understand

regimen: A plan for getting or staying healthy.

nutrition: The parts of food that your body uses to stay healthy.

nutritionist: A person who studies how food affects the body and what foods are best for it.

rejuvenate: Make something or someone feel or look fresher or younger.

metabolism: The chemical processes by which your body produces energy.

Chapter Three

NUTRITION FOR STRENGTH

When we look at a bodybuilder with huge muscles that are toned perfectly, we know that person not only followed a rigorous workout *regimen* but also regulated her diet. Achieving remarkable amounts of muscle mass requires intense amounts of discipline. The benefits of maintaining healthy *nutrition* are greater than making a bodybuilder strong; they also help lessen the chances of injury.

When the body trains, it breaks down and rebuilds muscle. Eating right is central to gaining muscle mass and staying healthy. Weightlifters must eat a proper blend of nutrients to make sure their bodies perform

Weightlifters should avoid foods with simple carbs like pasta made from white flour.

Weightlifting & Strength Building

as well as possible. Eating right doesn't just mean eating healthy foods, but also choosing when to eat, how much to eat, and whether to take dietary supplements. Eating healthy also does not mean eating *less*; in fact, the opposite can be true.

Of course, when you switch to a radically different diet or add nutritional supplements, you should consult a **nutritionist**, doctor, or other expert. Making up your own nutrition program can be dangerous.

WHAT TO EAT

While a balanced diet is important for everyone, it is even more important for athletes. An athlete eats considerably more than a non-active person. The average American eats 2000 calories a day, but an athlete who wants to gain large amounts of muscle mass could eat far more—between 3,000 and 4,000 calories—and continue to gain more muscle than fat.

You should consider three main food groups when choosing a diet for weightlifting: carbohydrates, protein and fats:

Carbohydrates provide energy to the body. Between 50 and 65 percent of an athlete's diet should be carbohydrates. Think of carbohydrates (also known simply as "carbs") as the fuel you need to keep your body running through workouts.

There are two types of carbohydrates: simple and complex. Simple carbohydrates break down faster and provide a burst of energy but then let your body down fast. Usually they are full of empty calories; they are foods that don't nourish the body but have a high amount of calories. Many teenagers love simple carbohydrate foods—candy, soda, and other sweets—but an athlete should avoid these foods. Some fruits, such as bananas, are simple carbohydrates and are filled with other vitamins and minerals as well as fiber, but bananas are an exception. While athletes should avoid empty-calorie foods at all times, they should especially steer clear of these foods before workouts to avoid a "crash"—a sudden lack of energy while they work out.

Complex carbohydrates break down more slowly in the body and provide it with more nutrients. Vegetables, fruits, brown rice, whole-grain

Soybeans are a good source of protein.

Weightlifting & Strength Building

bread, beans, nuts and cereal all contain complex carbohydrates. These complex carbohydrates give the body a more lasting boost of energy. Health professionals agree that switching from simple to complex carbohydrates is one of the smartest dietary choices a person can make. This can be as simple as buying whole-grain pasta instead of lighter kinds at the supermarket. Most complex carbohydrate foods are good sources of fiber, which makes the body feel more full, so you're less likely to crave junk food.

Proteins are important chemicals found in all living things. The chemicals are used to perform functions inside our body cells. Each protein is a long, folded, chain-like molecule make up of "links" called amino acids. Our bodies break down proteins found in foods and build new proteins that give the body the building blocks needed to form strong muscles. The best sources of proteins are meats, dairy products (like milk or cheese), eggs, and certain vegetables (such as soy beans and rice).

A good rule of thumb for knowing how much protein to eat is the number of grams should be equal to about one-third of your body weight in pounds. For example, a 200-pound person should eat about 70 grams of protein every day. Or a 120-pound person should have 40 grams of proteins.

When it comes to fat, people often think they should avoid it altogether—but fats actually help build up the body and can be used as sources of energy. Healthy teeth, skin, hair, and nerves all require a steady diet of fats. Fatty foods should make up no more than 25 percent of your caloric intake, however.

The kind of fat one consumes makes a difference; not all fats are alike. Fats can be classified as polyunsaturated, monounsaturated, and saturated fats. Unsaturated fat is good for the body, while saturated fats are best avoided. Monounsaturated fats (MUFA) such as those found in nuts, avocados, canola, and olive oil can even help contribute to weight loss. Polyunsaturated fats such as salmon, fish oil, corn, and soy help to lower cholesterol.

On the other hand, excessive fat intake can have negative effects,

Drink plenty of water while doing any kind of workout plan. Having water throughout the day instead of sugary sodas or juices is an easy, healthy change you can make right now!

Weightlifting & Strength Building

Make Connections

Keep these pointers in mind to make sure you're getting the right carbohydrates:

- Make half of your grains whole. Check the nutrition facts on bread, pasta and cereal. Make sure the word "whole" is in the first ingredient and avoid the word "enriched" on the back. Because complex carbohydrates are popular, labels misleadingly call foods whole grain when they are not.
- Eat five servings of fruit per day, and another five of vegetables.

especially if you're eating too much saturated fat. Meat, dairy, eggs, and seafood all contain saturated fats. Other oils such as coconut oil and palm oil also have "bad fat." Trans fats, created by scientists to preserve foods longer on the shelf, is a particularly bad form of fat. Many packaged foods like chips and microwavable popcorn contain trans fats. Fries from fast-food restaurants are commonly fried in trans fats. The health effects of eating trans fat are numerous and range from obesity and heart disease to infertility in women and even Alzheimer's. All these saturated fats contribute to a sluggish feeling after they are eaten. Any kind of fat takes from three to five hours to fully digest—so stock up on carbohydrates for energy instead of any fatty foods if you're planning to work out!

WATER

Water has been called the most important of all nutrients. The body is made up of 60 percent water, and all parts of the body depend on water to function. Water is so important that your body can only go for 48 hours without it, whereas if you had to, you could survive for weeks without food.

Text-Dependent Questions

1. What food groups are especially important for weightlifting?
2. Why are carbohydrates so important for athletes?
3. Explain the difference between complex and simple carbohydrates, and give examples of each.
4. What is protein? Give examples of foods that contain protein. How can you know how much protein you should be eating each day?
5. Describe two kinds of "good fat." What is an example of a "bad fat"?
6. Explain why water is so important to our bodies.

By hydrating (filling with water) ourselves, we *rejuvenate* all parts of our body, including the brain. Water transports nutrients around the body and helps regulate temperature and *metabolism*. You should drink water before, during, and after exercise. Weight lifters should drink eight glasses of water a day.

Drinking water actually makes you stronger, and even a small amount of dehydration can decrease strength by 15 percent. To maximize the intensity of workouts, an athlete needs to be hydrated. The whole process of muscle gain is aided by water, including breaking down muscle fiber in order to rebuild it stronger. Water also helps protect your joints by keeping them lubricated.

DIETARY SUPPLEMENTS

Weightlifters sometimes try to improve their performance by taking dietary supplements. These are pills or drinks that contain nutrients or chemicals to improve physical health or performance in the game. Dietary supplements do not include illegal performance-enhancing drugs.

Research Project

Use the Internet or library to find out more about dietary supplements that could help you build strength. What role does marketing play in how you perceive supplements? How can you sift through the advertising to determine the truth about supplements? Find reliable books or websites to answer the following questions: What kinds supplements are most trustworthy? Where and how are these supplements sold? What do they do for your body? Are there any supplements that are considered controversial or untrustworthy? What are they?

When properly used, supplements can improve overall health and performance. You should always consult a doctor or some other expert before taking them. Examples of common supplements include vitamin tablets, creatine, and protein shakes or powder.

Your body is capable of amazing things. Give it the right food—and then practice!

Words to Understand

monotonous: Repeated until it's boring.

cardiovascular: Having to do with your heart and blood vessels.

pecs: The large muscles that cover the ribcage.

traps: The large muscles covering the back of the neck and shoulder blades.

delts: A muscle that covers the shoulder joint, used for lifting the arms.

ligaments: Tough bands that connect bones together.

tendons: Tough, stretchy bands that connect muscles to bones.

stroke: A burst or blocked blood vessel in the brain.

synchronize: Do at the same time or in unison.

pliable: Easily bent; flexible.

groin: The region between your thighs, where your legs meet.

quadriceps: The muscles in the front of your upper leg.

hamstrings: The five powerful tendons at the back of a person's knee.

gluteals: The muscles in the buttocks.

Chapter Four

MAKING A PLAN TO BUILD STRENGTH WITH WEIGHTLIFTING

Weight training is an activity requiring mental discipline as much as physical discipline. One of the biggest challenges is to develop your strength gradually and safely, even when you are eager to push ahead quickly.

Injuries occur in weight training mainly because of careless technique or overly ambitious weight loading. Impatience is often the reason for this. Weight training has a rhythm to it. During the first six weeks of training—if you train regularly and properly—improvements to your physique can be quite rapid. Muscles in the arms, chest, and shoulders will tone and strengthen, and you may find you lose some weight. After

As you work out more, you'll build more strength and have to start lifting larger weights. Choosing the right weight to push yourself while not risking injury is an important part of building strength over time in a healthy way.

44   Weightlifting & Strength Building

Make Connections

 Repeating the same action many times causes an overuse or chronic injury. This is not as serious as the kind of injury that happens suddenly, but any chronic problem may become worse if not acknowledged early on, so weight lifters should seek medical advice and treatment. Overuse injuries have both mental and physical symptoms:

* unusual tiredness or fatigue
* a lack of appetite
* an inability to sleep at night
* muscle soreness and cramps
* stiff, painful or unstable joints
* problems getting part of the body comfortable in bed at night
* painful tendons
* pain that shows no improvement after three days.

But do not treat every ache and pain that follows weight training as an injury. Any sport may result in a phenomenon known as delayed-onset muscle soreness. It's caused by the healing of those tiny tears in the muscle tissue that were incurred during training. Usually the ache will disappear within forty-eight hours. However, if it persists for more than three days, you should see a doctor. Remember to drink plenty of water before, during, and after your weight training session. This helps muscles lose their soreness after exercise because they will rehydrate quicker.

this period, progress becomes slower. As your body strengthens, you will need to work harder to continue developing muscles.

When you struggle to put on more muscle, several things can happen. You may simply become discouraged and stop training. To counter this, focus on the improvements to your fitness rather than improvements to your appearance. However much you develop your muscles, there will always be someone bigger and more toned.

If your only reason for doing weight training is to look good, ask yourself whether there is a deeper reason. Do you want people to respect you more? Do you want more attention from the opposite sex? You may have a poor self-image. Work out what it is you really want; simply putting on muscle bulk is unlikely to solve problems with self-image. Concentrate on the improvements in how you feel rather than on how you look. Enjoy the fact that you are getting fitter and stronger, and treat improvements in appearance as a bonus.

Of course, the other reason you might stop training is boredom. Weight training can be repetitive and *monotonous*, and if you are not seeing muscle gain, you may feel like giving up. There are several things you can do to stop weight training from becoming boring:

- Vary your routines at the gym. If you concentrate on doing upper-body workouts one day, switch the next day to lower-body workouts, or spend more time on the *cardiovascular* machines.
- Shorten your workouts on some days. After a proper warm-up, you can do weights for just fifteen minutes and still get the benefit. In that time, you can do several exercises to work your legs, lats, *pecs*, *traps*, *delts*, and abdominals. Short routines are not for every time you go to the gym, but just for now and then, on those days when you really want to be somewhere else.
- Plan an enjoyable activity with your training partner for after the weights session. Following training with something exciting can make the training more exciting.

STEADY TRAINING

Weight training cannot be rushed. Do not make large jumps in the weights used. Adding ten pounds to your weight stack when you already struggle at the level where you are is a recipe for torn muscles, *ligaments*, and *tendons*. It can even result in a *stroke*. Furthermore, do not over train by visiting the gym more often. During weight training, muscle fibers suffer microscopic tears from the effort. The fibers heal themselves, becoming stronger than they were before, during periods of rest. If you do not have at least one day of rest between training days, this healing and muscle development cannot take place. Therefore, your muscles will be more likely to be injured during training.

People under the age of eighteen should follow these training rules:

- Do not train more than three times a week.
- Keep training sessions under forty-five minutes—ideally closer to thirty minutes.
- When you first start on a particular machine or free-weights exercise, practice the technique lifting no weight at all. Then lift weights under expert supervision until you can demonstrate perfect technique in up to fifteen repetitions.
- According to sports medicine experts Avery Faigenbaum and Wayne Westcott, the young weightlifter should add weights in increments of 1 to 3 pounds and perform one to three sets at the new weight. Once she can demonstrate perfect technique at the new weight, she may add further weights.

Another important ingredient for safe training is concentration. Whenever you lift, pull, or push a weight, focus all your attention on the muscle groups doing the work. If, for instance, you are doing a biceps curl exercise on a machine, concentrate on the slow curling action of your arms up toward our chest and then the release back down to the starting position. Feel what the muscles are doing throughout the lift, and move only your forearms; the rest of your body should be entirely still. To aid your concentration, *synchronize* your breathing with the action. Do not hold your breath, (which is a common mistake) because this deprives muscles of vital oxygen needed to work. Breathe out as you lift the weights to your chest, and inhale as you lower them. Maintaining concentration throughout a lift helps protect you from injuries caused by poor technique.

Stretching before and after each workout is the best way to avoid injury.

WARMING UP AND STRETCHING

Before each session of weight training, you have to prepare the body in order to reduce the risks of injury. Do this in two stages: warming up and stretching.

Some people arrive in a gym and rush straight to their favorite weight machine, lifting as much weight as they can. They are heading for the doctor. Weight training with cold and stiff muscles is a recipe for quick injury, mainly sprains and strains. Doing a proper warm-up routine will prepare your body for training. In turn, this means that each weight session will bring more progress.

A warm-up routine does exactly what it says—warms up the muscles, ligaments, and tendons of the body in preparation for exercise. A warm muscle is more **pliable** and flexible than a cold muscle, which means you can put it through an extended range of movement without damaging it.

Muscles also rely on oxygen to give them energy to work. Oxygen is carried to the muscles in the blood, and the blood picks up the oxygen as it passes through the lungs. During a warm-up routine, both breathing and heart rate are increased by light exercise. The overall effect is that we breathe in more air; more oxygen is delivered to the blood; and the blood pumps faster through the body.

A basic warm-up routine involves light exercise for between five and ten minutes, just enough to get slightly out of breath, raise the heartbeat, and warm up muscles. The key rule of a warm-up is not to do anything too strenuous but merely to prepare the muscles for exercise. Here is a typical warm-up routine:

1. Run very lightly on the spot without raising your knees too high. Shake your arms loosely by your sides to get rid of any stiffness in the arms and shoulders. Run for about two to three minutes, slightly increasing the pace and the height you raise the knees.

2. Stand up straight with your legs shoulder width apart, looking straight ahead. Swing your arms forward in large circles about ten times, and then reverse the direction of the circles. Finally, swing the arms inward across your chest so that they cross each other, then outward again. Repeat ten times. This will warm up your shoulders.

3. To warm up your muscles, make large circles with your head in one direction about five times. Then reverse the direction for another five times. Brush the chest with your chin at the lowest point of the circle and stretch your head up rather than back at the top of the circle.

4. To warm up the leg and knee muscles, do about two minutes of lunges—stepping forward and then back with one leg, and repeating with the other. Do not push too hard, and make sure you

Making a Plan   49

bend your thigh so that it is at about a forty-five-degree angle to the floor.

5. Make large circles with your hips, first in one direction and then in the other. The circles should be as wide as possible, with your hands placed on your hips to facilitate the movement.

6. Finally, shake your entire body to loosen up and complete the warm-up. This warm-up does not use machines. In a gym you can warm up on some of the warm-up machines. The rowing machine, treadmill, stepper, and track machine (which imitates a skiing action) are all suitable. Try to combine two machines with different actions so that you warm up your entire body. A good combination would be the rowing machine and the stepper. Whatever machine you use, start at a gentle pace and work only hard enough to raise your breathing and temperature.

Once you have finished your warm-up, you can proceed to stretching. Flexibility is essential for almost every sport, including weight training. A weight-training session should work all the major muscle groups of the body so your flexibility preparation must do the same.

There are a huge number of different stretches you can do. Ask a qualified sports coach, yoga teacher, or a similar flexibility expert to teach you a broad range of techniques. Organize these into a specific routine that you will use before every weight-training session. Work from your feet to your head, or vice versa, so that you do not miss any muscles. It is important that you stretch any injured muscles or ligaments, until they are fully healed.

Here is a basic stretching routine:

1. Seated hamstring stretch: sit on the floor with your legs stretched out in front of you and your back straight. Breathe in and bend forward from the waist until you can grip your ankles. Holding onto your ankles, bend farther forward until you feel a stretch along the calf muscles and the back of the knee. Hold the position before about ten seconds and then sit up slowly.

2. Quadriceps stretch: stand up straight, resting one hand against a

Make Connections

If you answer yes to any of the following questions, you should have a medical checkup before beginning any program of weight training.

- Have you suffered from any sort of heart condition that stopped you from doing physical exercise?
- Do you suffer from asthma?
- Are you on any medication for an existing illness?
- Have you suffered serious injury or illness affecting your spine, neck, bones, or certain body joints?
- Have you ever experienced any chest pains during physical activity?
- Do you suffer from periods of dizziness or fainting?
- Do you have epilepsy or any other condition that results in seizures or loss of consciousness?
- Do you have any other medical condition that might affect your ability to exercise?

wall for stability. Lift up your left leg behind you, then take hold of the top of the foot with your left hand and pull the heel up toward your buttocks. You should feel the stretch along the front of the thigh and the knee. Hold the position for about thirty seconds, then let go of the foot and return to the floor. Repeat this exercise with your right leg.

3. *Groin* stretch: sit on the floor and draw your feet into the groin, pressing the soles of the feet together so that the knees fall outward. Take hold of your ankles with your hands, and push down on the knees using your elbows. The stretch is concentrated along the inside of the groin. Hold the stretch for about twenty seconds, then gently release the pressure on your knees and bring them up to the center.

4. Side stretch: stand with your legs in an "A" shape two shoulder-widths apart. Keeping your back straight, slide your left hand down the side of your left leg as far as you can. Once you have reached your maximum position, hold it for five seconds, and then slowly come up again to the middle. Then repeat the exercise on the right side. Repeat the set three times.

5. Waist and backstretch: again stand with your legs in an "A" shape two shoulder-widths apart. Bend straight forward from the waist and lower your torso as far as it will go, keeping your back straight. Holding the legs and gently pulling on them will help you to go down farther. Hold the stretch for about ten seconds, and then move your body upright again. Place your hands against your lower back and stretch your body backward, looking up at the ceiling as you do. Hold for ten seconds, then release.

6. Shoulder stretch: hold your left arm straight out in front of you and hook your right forearm around the back of the left elbow. Keeping the left arm straight, use the right arm to pull it across your body until you feel a strong stretch in the shoulder joint. Hold for ten seconds, then release and switch arms.

7. Neck stretch: standing up straight, lower your chin so that it rests against your chest. You should feel a stretch up the back of your neck. Hold for five seconds, then release. Next, bend your head backward and look up toward the ceiling. Do not let your head fall too far backward because this can damage the top vertebrae. Instead, feel you are stretching your face up toward the ceiling. Hold for five seconds and release. Finally, twist your head to look left and then right, each time holding the stretch for five seconds.

SAFE WEIGHT TRAINING

Many weight-training injuries come from misuse of equipment and the wrong type of training. For anyone younger than eighteen, incorrect technique or weight selection can have a very harmful long-term effect on the growing body.

Make Connections

Do not wear jewelry when weight training, particularly neck-laces, rings, and earrings. As well as being a hazard to you, some jewelry—especially rings—can stretch or damage the handles of equipment.

- Do not wear excessively baggy T-shirts, which can get caught in machinery. If you are using the rowing machine, tuck your T-shirt into the waistband of your shorts or gym pants to prevent them from getting caught in the runners.

- If using free weights, place them back on the free-weights rack in the same order in which they were arranged. If you have added weights to a bar, it is polite to remove them after use.

- Never leave any litter in the gym, and make sure all bags and personal belongings are safely out of the way.

- When using weight machines, wear good-quality training shoes with rubber nonskid soles to prevent slipping.

Many experts frown on the idea of weight training for people under the age of eighteen. The main concern is that loading the still-growing body with heavy weight can deform and damage it, leaving the young person with injuries that last a lifetime. Young people have several important physiological differences from adults, all of which relate to the process of growing. First, during periods of growth, muscles and cartilage are at an increased risk of injury as they stretch to cope with the lengthening of the body. Second, growth makes body joints unstable because muscles around the joints are also adjusting to growth. Finally, the skeleton itself is stretching. In the long bones of the body (such as those that are found in the legs and arms), there are "growth plates," special sections of the bone that enable it to lengthen properly. Loading the growing bones with excessive weight can deform these growth plates and lead to permanent bone damage. Similarly, the growing spine is more likely to be injured and distorted under heavy weights.

Though these cautions are extremely important, they do not mean that you should never do weight training. Safe weight training for those under eighteen is a matter of learning the correct technique and avoiding dangerous exercises.

For young people, the recommended frequency of weight training is two to three sessions per week. Two is the ideal number because it lets you do other forms of exercise during the week. Mixing weight training with sports such as running, swimming, and basketball is also recommended because cross training provides an all-around level of fitness, which helps guard against injury. Doing only weight training may be too hard on your bones, joints, and muscles.

Adult bodybuilders will attempt to lift the heaviest weights possible as part of their routines. Do NOT attempt this if you are under eighteen; your body is not yet strong enough to support extremely concentrated weight stacks. Gauge the right level of weight for you by the number of repetitions. If you cannot lift, pull, or push a weight with proper technique for eight consecutive repetitions, it is too heavy for you. Instead of aiming to lift large weights, focus on increasing the number of repetitions you do with a weight you can lift comfortably, two sets per exercise.

Steer clear of dead lifts. Dead lifts involve lifting a heavy barbell weight without using a bench, seat, or other support to stabilize you. Your body will undergo dangerous stress during a dead lift, as different muscles throughout the body attempt to keep their balance under the sudden weight.

All weight training should be done slowly and methodically. When lifting, never snatch or jerk the weight. Instead, move it steadily from the start position to the stop position, and always go through the full range of body motion for the exercise. This is where good technique makes a difference.

Do not use any machine or attempt any new free-weight lift until an expert has coached you in it. Free weights are especially dangerous.

Not only are more muscles required for balance when lifting a free weight, but incorrect technique may result in dropping the weight on yourself as well. This last danger is one reason why you should always have a spotter with you when you attempt free-weight lifting.

Some basic principles of technique are applicable to almost all weight-training exercises. These involve how you stand, sit, bend, and breathe. Posture is extremely important in weight training. For example, if you sit in a slouching position while performing an overhead press exercise, the spine is placed under unnatural pressure, like a stick being bent until it snaps. If you sit straight, however, the vertebrae of the spine distribute the pressure evenly and naturally. To achieve the proper sitting position, push your buttocks to the very back of the seat and keep your back straight. Lift your chin up, and pull your shoulders back to avoid slouching. Your feet must be flat on the floor and slightly back toward your thighs.

Note that the correct upper-body sitting position is also the correct upper-body standing and bending position. Learning how to sit and stand properly is valuable because it affects your ability to handle weights safely. For example, a popular weight training exercise is the barbell squat. Here, a barbell is held behind the neck and across the shoulders, using an overhand grip. With the weight in this position, the **quadriceps, hamstrings**, and **gluteals** are exercised by slowly bending the knees until the thighs are parallel to the floor, and then slowly returning to the start position. During this exercise, the back needs to be kept as upright as possible, with the head up and face looking forward; otherwise, the spine will take the pressure of the exercise rather than the leg muscles.

Bending to pick up or handle any weight must be done from the legs and not the back. Try this exercise: place any object (it need not be heavy) on the floor. Stand with your feet close to it and your back straight. Look directly forward. Now bend from your knees and lower yourself down beside the object. At the same time, keep your back as straight as possible. Once you have taken hold of the object, lift your face and look straight forward—this helps to keep your back upright.

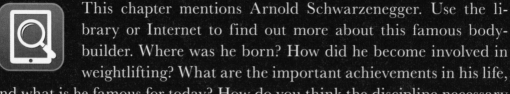
Complete the lift by using your legs to push the weight from the floor. If the weight is heavy, keep it close to your stomach, the body's natural center of gravity.

If you are going to take weight training seriously, protecting your back will save you from many problems. Get into the habit of sitting, standing, and bending properly at all times, and those habits will transfer into the gym.

Correct breathing is as much a part of good technique as correct posture. Strong breathing maintains the supply of oxygen to the muscles while they are working. The problem with the way many of us breathe is that we do not use our lungs to full capacity. This results in a poor input of oxygen to the body. Worse still, while exerting ourselves we have the tendency to hold our breath. This is dangerous during weight training because the combination of held breath and muscular exertion cuts off oxygen in the brain, possibly resulting in a stroke. It is important to learn proper full-lung breathing. Draw in a deep breathe through your nose. Imagine that you are pulling the breath into your stomach; you will notice that your abdomen inflates first, and then the chest. This sequence indicates that the whole of the lung from bottom to top is filled with air. Exhale from your mouth; the chest will collapse first, followed by the stomach.

Use deep breathing throughout your weight training. However, make sure you follow a specific rhythm. When you lift, pull, or push the weight (known as the "power phase"), breathe out. When you relax the weight back to its starting position, breathe in. This sequence keeps you from holding your breath. The power phase of an exercise should take three full seconds to complete, as should the return phase. Count this rhythm mentally by saying, "one elephant, two elephants, three elephants." Using the word "elephant" ensures that you count in complete seconds. Counting in this way prevents you from using those rapid, jerky movements that are so apt to result in an injury.

If you're just starting to think about a fitness program that's right for you, you may think that strength training is only for experienced athletes. But you don't have to be Arnold Schwarzenegger to reap the benefits of weightlifting! Strength training has too many physical, health, and mental benefits to leave it out of your workout schedule. Why not give it a try?

FIND OUT MORE

In Books

Everett, Greg. *Olympic Weightlifting: A Complete Guide for Athletes and Coaches.* Sunnyvale, Calif.: Catalyst Athletics, 2009.

Delavier, Frederic. *Strength Training Anatomy.* Champagne, Ill.: Human Kinetics, 2010.

Rippetoe, Mark. *Starting Strength.* Wichita Falls, Tex.: Aasgaard, 2011.

Schuler, Lou and Cassandra Forsythe. *The New Rules of Lifting for Women: Lift Like a Man, Look Like a Goddess.* New York: Avery, 2008.

Takano, Bob. *Weightlifting Programming: A Winning Coach's Guide.* Sunnyvale, Calif.: Catalyst Athletics, 2012.

Online

Beginner Weight-Training Guide
www.bodybuilding.com/fun/beginner_weight_training.htm

Beginner Weight-Training Workout Routine
www.aworkoutroutine.com/the-beginner-weight-training-workout-routine

Strength Training
kidshealth.org/teen/food_fitness/exercise/strength_training.html

Strength Training for Beginners
www.fitnessmagazine.com/workout/lose-weight/build-strength/
strength-training-for-beginners

Strength Training OK for Kids?
www.mayoclinic.org/strength-training/art-20047758

SERIES GLOSSARY OF KEY TERMS

abs: Short for abdominals. The muscles in the middle of your body, located over your stomach and intestines.

aerobic: A process by which energy is steadily released using oxygen. Aerobic exercise focuses on breathing and exercising for a long time.

anaerobic: When lots of energy is quickly released, without using oxygen. You can't do anaerobic exercises for a very long time.

balance: Your ability to stay steady and upright.

basal metabolic rate: How many calories your body burns naturally just by breathing and carrying out other body processes.

bodybuilding: Exercising specifically to get bigger, stronger muscles.

calories: The units of energy that your body uses. You get calories from food and you use them up when you exercise.

carbohydrates: The foods that your body gets most of its energy from. Common foods high in carbohydrates include sugars and grains.

cardiovascular system: Your heart and blood vessels.

circuit training: Rapidly switching from one exercise to another in a cycle. Circuit training helps build endurance in many different muscle groups.

circulatory system: The system of blood vessels in your body, which brings oxygen and nutrients to your cells and carries waste products away.

cool down: A gentle exercise that helps your body start to relax after a workout.

core: The muscles of your torso, including your abs and back muscles.

cross training: When an athlete trains for a sport she normally doesn't play, to exercise any muscle groups she might be weak in.

dehydration: When you don't have enough water in your body. When you exercise, you lose water by sweating, and it's important to replace it.

deltoids: The thick muscles covering your shoulder joint.

energy: The power your body needs to do things like move around and keep you alive.

endurance: The ability to keep going for a long time.

flexibility: How far you can bend, or how far your muscles can stretch.

glutes: Short for gluteals, the muscles in your buttocks.

hydration: Taking in more water to keep from getting dehydrated.

isometric: An exercise that you do without moving, by holding one position.

isotonic: An exercise you do by moving your muscles.

lactic acid: A chemical that builds up in your muscles after you exercise. It causes a burning feeling during anaerobic exercises.

lats: Short for latissimus dorsi, the large muscles along your back.

metabolism: How fast you digest food and burn energy.

muscle: The parts of your body that contract and expand to allow you to move.

nervous system: Made up of your brain, spinal cord, and nerves, which carry messages between your brain, spinal cord, and the rest of your body.

nutrition: The chemical parts of the food you eat that your body needs to survive and use energy.

obliques: The muscles to either side of your stomach, under your ribcage.

pecs: Short for pectorals, the muscles on your chest.

quads: Short for quadriceps, the large muscle on the front of your upper leg and thigh.

reps: How many times you repeat an anaerobic exercise in a row.

strength: The power of your muscles.

stretching: Pulling on your muscles to make them longer. Stretching before you exercise can keep you flexible and prevent injuries.

warm up: A light exercise you do before a workout to get your body ready for harder exercise.

weight training: Exercises that involve lifting heavy weights to increase your strength and endurance.

INDEX

aerobic 11, 17, 21
amino acids 37
anaerobic 11, 21

barbell 15, 24–25, 54–55
blood 42, 49
bodybuilding 17–21
bones 13, 21, 42, 51, 53–54
breathing 11, 47, 49–50, 56–57

calories 11, 35
carbohydrates 35, 37, 39–40
clean and jerk 15, 17, 21
concentration 47

dead lifts 20, 54
diet 11, 33, 35, 37
dumbbell 25

endorphins 11
exercise bench 24–25

fat 11, 35, 37, 39–40
flexibility 50
free weights 23–27, 29, 31, 53–55

gym 15, 19–20, 27–29, 31, 46, 48, 50, 53, 56

heart 11, 17, 39, 42, 49, 51

injuries 33, 43–45, 47–48, 51–54, 57
International Federation of Body Building (IFBB) 19
International Powerlifting Federation (IPF) 20–21
International Weightlifting Federation (IWF) 15

joint 9, 40, 42, 45, 51–54

ligaments 42, 46, 49–50

muscle 9–13, 15, 17, 19, 21–23, 25, 27, 31, 33, 35, 37, 40, 42–43, 45–50, 53–56
myofibrils 11, 13

nutrition 32–33, 35, 39

Olympic 9, 14–16, 19
oxygen 11, 47, 49, 56

pain 45
powerlifting 20–21
posture 55–56
protein 35–37, 40–41

safety 29
Sinclair Coefficient 17

snatch 15, 17, 21, 54
spotter 27, 55
stress 11, 54
stretching 48, 50, 52–53, 57
stroke 42, 46, 56
supplements 35, 40–41

tendon 42, 45–46, 49

warm-up 46, 48–50, 57
water 38–40, 45
weight machine 23, 25–27, 29, 31, 48, 53

ABOUT THE AUTHOR AND THE CONSULTANT

Celicia Scott lives in upstate New York. She worked in teaching before starting a second career as a writer.

Diane H. Hart, Nationally Certified Fitness Professional and Health Specialist, has designed and implemented fitness and wellness programs for more than twenty years. She is a master member of the International Association of Fitness Professionals, and a health specialist for Blue Shield of Northeastern New York, HealthNow, and Palladian Health. In 2010, Diane was elected president of the National Association for Health and Fitness (NAHF), a nonprofit organization that exists to improve the quality of life for individuals in the United States through the promotion of physical fitness, sports, and healthy lifestyles. NAHF accomplishes this work by fostering and supporting state governors and state councils and coalitions that promote and encourage regular physical activity. NAHF is also the national sponsor of Employee Health and Fitness Month, the largest global workplace health and fitness event each May. American College of Sports Medicine (ACSM) has been a strategic partner with NAHF since 2009.

PICTURE CREDITS

MERIDIAN MIDDLE SCHOOL
2195 Brandywyn Lane
Buffalo Grove, IL 60089

DATE DUE

DEMCO, INC. 38-2931